THE OLD WOMAN
AND
HER PIG

A picture book

grant and griffith

[ZHINGOORA BOOKS]

THE OLD WOMAN AND HER PIG.

A little old woman, who lived in a house,

Too small for a giant, too big for a mouse,—

Was sweeping her chambers, (though she
had not many,)

When she found, by good fortune, a bright silver penny!

Delighted she seized it, and, dancing a jig,

Exclaim'd, "With this money I'll purchase a pig."

So saying, away to the market she went,

And the fruits of her fortunate sweeping she spent

On a smooth-coated, black-spotted, curly-tailed thing,

Which she led off in triumph, by means of a string.

But how shall I paint her vexation and toil,

When, in crossing a meadow, she came to a
stile,

And found neither threats nor persuasions
would do

To induce Mr. Piggy to climb or creep
through?

She coax'd him, she strok'd him, she patted
his hide,

She scolded him, threaten'd him, thump'd
him beside;

But coaxing, and scolding, and thumping
proved vain,

Whilst the evening grew dark, and 'twas likely
to rain.

The dame, out of patience, now cried, in a fright,

To a dog which came up, "Pray, give Piggy a bite,

"And over the stile, Sir, compel him to go,

"Or here I may stay till 'tis midnight, you know."

This request Mr. Bow-wow, of course, must have heard,

But he silently stood, without saying a word.

"Well, well," said the dame, "I'll be even with you,—

"Unkindness like this you may happen to rue."

Then pausing and anxiously looking around,

She saw a stout crab-stick lie flat on the ground.

"Kind stick," she exclaim'd, "I entreat you to flog

"This cruel, regardless, unmannerly dog,

"Who will not bite Piggy, though plainly you see

"My pig will not stir, and there's no home for me."

No reply made the stick, not a blow would it strike,

But crab-stick and cur remained silent alike.

"Well, this is provoking! but yonder's a fire,

"And now," said old Goody, "I'll have my
desire."

The flame she saluted, and cried, "Pray be
quick,

"Assist a poor woman, and burn this vile stick,

"For 'twill not beat yon dog, though the cur
will not bite

"My pig; and I here may remain all the night."

In vain to the flame did our sweeper appeal,

For her sufferings it would not, or
perhaps *could not*, feel.

An opposite element next caught her eye,

And its friendly assistance she therefore
would try.—

"Dear water," she said, "do extinguish this
fire,

"Which will not (although 'tis my ardent
desire)

"Consume yonder crab-stick, which, obstinate
too,

"With beating that cur will have nothing to
do;

8"And the dog, as ill-natured, you see, as the
rest,

"Refuses to bite this young obstinate beast;

"So here I'm compelled, most reluctant, to
stay,

"And here may remain till the break of the
day."

The water regardless of all that was said,

Lay perfectly still,—not an effort was made.

So next to an ox her attention she turn'd,

And telling him how her entreaties were
scorned,

9By the dog, by the stick, by the flame, and the flood,

She said, "I beseech you, great Sir, be so good,

"As to drink up this water, which, every one knows,

"Could have put out the fire with ease, if it chose:

"Oh grant me this favour—do pity my plight,

"Or here in the fields I must stay all the night!"

The ox was unmoved, not an eye would he turn,

Though no flood would extinguish, no fire would burn,

No crab-stick would give Mr. Bow-wow a blow,

Nor would he compel the pig forward to go.

Then kindling with rage Piggy's mistress cried out,

"Oh! here comes a man, he'll avenge me no doubt."

So once more relating her pitiful story,

She said, "In the death of that ox I should glory:

10"Now therefore, good butcher, the animal kill;

"I'll thank you, I'll bless you; indeed, Sir, I will."

The butcher, however, continued his way,

Without even deigning one sentence to say.

Goody trembled with rage; yet she ventured to hope

A friend was at hand, when she saw a new rope.

So now with clasp'd hands, mournful voice, and bent knees,

She said, "Hang that butcher, good rope, if you please;

"For, though his lawful vocation each day,

"An ox the barbarian refuses to slay."

She paused for an answer; but hard was her lot,

No help, nor a word of reply could be got.

A veteran rat at this moment drew near,

And quietly stood her entreaties to hear.

So curtseying low,—"I entreat," said the
dame,

"By your grandfather's beard and your
grandmother's fame,

"By the conquests your father and uncles
have won,

"And the deeds which both you and your
brethren have done,

"That your worship will not disappoint my
fond hope,

"But graciously gnaw and destroy yonder
rope,

"Which, spite of a moving and melting
harangue,

"Refuses that obstinate butcher to hang."

But ah! in the rat no assistance was found,

And Goody's last hope seemed to fall to the
ground.

But now kind dame Fortune at length
interfered,

And a fierce-looking cat in a moment
appear'd;

A cat which was hungry, and ready to slay,

For supper, whatever might come in his way.

No sooner had, therefore, old Goody repeated

The slights with which all her petitions were treated,

Than Mr. Grimalkin, espousing her cause,

Seiz'd the ill-natured rat in his terrible claws;

"O spare me!" he squeaked, "and the rope I'll destroy;"

But when he began his sharp teeth to employ,

The rope to hang up the cross butcher prepar'd;

And the butcher, that moment, most terribly scar'd,

At the head of the ox aim'd a death-giving blow;

But submission is better than death we all know:

So away, at full speed, the wise animal ran

To drink up the water.—The water began

The flame to extinguish: but now 'twas the turn

Of the fire the ill-natured crab-stick to burn.

"Hold, hold," said the stick, "I am going to flog,

"Most soundly that obstinate cur of a dog."

"But, Sir," said the dog, in a terrible fright,

"The old lady's pig I'm preparing to bite."

This proved to be true, and his bite was
severe:

"Oh, oh!" cried the pig, "I must not remain here;"

So over the stile he thought proper to get,

And Goody no more had occasion to fret;

For the pig to his sty was now easily led,

And she put him a trough, and clean straw for a bed:

16Then fastened the door and wish'd him good night.

The pig gave a grunt, as he could not speak right.

The old dame went into her neat little house,

And is now safe in bed, and as snug as a mouse.

End of the book.